FAMOUS FAMILIES™

GOLDIE HAWN AND KATE HUDSON

LISA MODIFICA

The Rosen Publishing Group, Inc., New York

To cool, smart women, wherever they are

Published in 2005 by The Rosen Publishing Group, Inc.
29 East 21st Street, New York, NY 10010

First Edition

Library of Congress Cataloging-in-Publication Data

Modifica, Lisa.
Goldie Hawn and Kate Hudson / Lisa Modifica.—1st ed.
    p. cm. — (Famous families)
Includes bibliographical references and index.
ISBN 1-4042-0259-5 (library binding)
1. Hawn, Goldie. 2. Hudson, Kate, 1979– 3. Motion picture actors and actresses—United States—Biography.
I. Title. II. Series.
PN2287.H334M64 2004
791.4302'8'092273—dc22

2004015543

Manufactured in the United States of America

Contents

A FAMOUS FAMILY

Famous families are always interesting. We see celebrities and stars on television or in the movies, and we can't help but wonder what their lives are like in private. When there is more than one famous person in a family, it's even more interesting. What do Brad Pitt and Jennifer Aniston do when they are at home? Do they cook and watch television like the rest of us?

Unfortunately, famous families often have a lot of problems. Living in the spotlight is hard. People are constantly following celebrities and telling lies about things they said or did. Famous couples often break up under the pressure of always being watched.

One inspirational famous family is the mother-daughter team of Goldie Hawn and Kate Hudson. Goldie is a world-famous actress, producer, writer, and director, and Kate is an actress who has become famous in the past few years. Both mother and daughter won major awards while in their twenties, and both are around for the long term. Their family is even more impressive when you add that Kurt Russell, another major movie star, is Goldie's partner and has lived with the family for more than twenty years.

In 2000, Goldie and Kate hosted the 24th annual Crystal Awards luncheon. This prestigious award ceremony honors Canada's most talented women in the film and television industry. At the luncheon, Goldie and Kate paid tribute to Nikki Rocco, the first woman to head a major studio distribution operation, as well as Barbara Boyle, a famous producer.

Pictured here are Goldie Hawn and Kurt Russell. As well as being a very successful actor, Kurt had a baseball career for a short while. He also performs many of his movie stunts himself. Baseball is a Russell family tradition: Kurt's father and nephew both played professionally.

Goldie and Kate are refreshing because they are both positive, down-to-earth women who support each other. These qualities are often hard to find in famous actresses. In interviews, Goldie always talks about how great her family is. And Kate always mentions how supportive Goldie and Kurt were while she was growing up. Kurt is Goldie's live-in partner. He has acted like a father to Kate since she was four. In 2001, Kate told *ABC News*, "No matter what any of us did, [Goldie and Kurt] were completely supportive and wanted us to do what we wanted to do, as long as we were dedicated to it, and we had a strong work ethic."

Kate's Dreams

Kate says she has always wanted to act. Since she was a child, she told anyone who would listen that one day she would be in film. Goldie and Kurt always made it clear that Kate should finish high school before starting an acting career. When Kate was sixteen years old, Kurt was working on an action movie called *Escape from L.A.* Kurt and his partners on the film had been looking for an actress to play a character in the movie for weeks. Kate remembers Kurt coming to her and telling her that she was perfect for the part and that she should audition. Kate auditioned for *Escape from L.A.* and got the part (eventually, however, she turned it down).

As Kate remembers, it all happened so fast. She doesn't remember whether her mother was in London or Paris at the time, but she remembers that she was away working. After Kate had called to tell her mom she got a part in *Escape from L.A.*, Goldie got on the next plane home. Kate remembers that they sat down to talk about her plans. Kate told Goldie she definitely wanted to act. As she recalls, "Mum [mom] just sorta went—OK, if this is what you want to do, you [need to] start thinking straight. I did and ever since I make choices that I felt were, you know, good choices."

Kate often tells interviewers that Goldie and Kurt didn't pressure her into acting, but when she decided she wanted to act, they fully supported her. She is lucky to have such a nurturing family.

CHAPTER 1

MAKING IT BIG

Goldie Hawn is a living legend. Few actresses have been popular for the amount of time she has. Goldie believes she has been around so long because she works very hard and tries to make decisions based on who she is and what she believes instead of what will make her more popular or rich. People who work with Goldie have only positive things to say. Goldie is constantly described as beautiful, funny, intelligent, and kind.

Goldie, or rather Goldie Studlendgehawn, was born on November 21, 1945, in Washington, D.C. Goldie grew up in a Maryland suburb and began dance lessons at age three. At ten, she debuted as a dancer in *The Nutcracker* in Virginia and continued performing in local plays and musicals. At seventeen, she was managing a local dance studio and studying drama at American University.

At age seventeen, Goldie joined summer stock in Williamsburg, Virginia. Summer stock is a group of actors who perform in the same theater throughout the summer. Goldie played Juliet in Shakespeare's *Romeo and Juliet*. She has said that it was one of the greatest moments in her career. "3,000 people in

In this headshot of Goldie, taken in the 1970s, the strong family resemblance between mother and daughter is obvious. Kate Hudson, born at the end of the 1970s, grew up to have not only her mother's smile but also her beauty, toughness, and independent spirit.

the amphitheatre, it rained, and nobody moved. My dad came backstage trying not to cry. He looked at me, he said, 'Go, [short for Goldie] where did you learn to do that?'"

In 1964, Goldie moved to New York and performed cancan dancing at the New York World's Fair. Cancan is a type of dance in which a line of women kick up their legs while wearing fluffy, colorful skirts. In New York, Goldie worked as a dancer in clubs and in musicals. In 1967, she moved to Los Angeles, California, and got a spot dancing on a comedic variety show hosted by Andy Griffith. A casting agent saw her and cast her as a gossipy neighbor in a TV series called *Good Morning World*. The series lasted only a season, but Goldie was noticed by an agent who got her a part on Rowan and Martin's *Laugh-In*.

Laugh-In was a popular variety show that aired from 1968 to 1973, and Goldie became an audience favorite. Originally, she danced on the show, but she was soon given speaking lines and it became obvious that she had a talent for comedy. Her character wore a bikini and had words and symbols written on her body. On *Laugh-In*, Goldie was famous for getting her lines wrong and laughing about it. It all started when she mixed up a line and started to laugh hysterically. The director left Goldie's blooper in the show when it went on air, and the audience loved it. Eventually, the *Laugh-In* crew started holding Goldie's cue cards upside down so she would mess up her lines and laugh. Most viewers were introduced to Goldie's bubbly, upbeat personality on *Laugh-In*.

Goldie's unusual name as well as her cheerful and fun personality run in her family. She shares her first name with a great-aunt and a cousin. Here, as the only real blonde Goldie in her family (at least so far), she poses for a late 1960s publicity shot in a bikini and covered in body paint.

This still from the 1969 film *Cactus Flower* shows Goldie starring as the character Toni Simmons. In keeping with 1960s' style, the film's tagline was "*Cactus Flower* has flower power."

In 1968, Goldie acted and danced in her first feature film, *The One and Only, Genuine, Original Family Band*. Kurt Russell was also in the film. Neither of them had any idea that later in life they would become a couple. A year later, Goldie starred in *Cactus Flower*, which turned out to be her breakthrough role. *Cactus Flower* was originally a popular play. In the film, actor Walter Matthau plays a dentist who is dating Toni, played by Goldie.

The dentist is single but tells Toni that he is married to avoid a serious relationship. Eventually, he tells Toni he will marry her. Toni does not want to break up his marriage and insists on meeting his wife. The dentist convinces his nurse,

An Artistic Family

Goldie Hawn's mother was a dancer, and her father was a violinist.

played by Ingrid Bergman, to pretend she's married to him. All kinds of funny twists and turns follow, as the dentist tells more lies. The film was very popular, and audiences and critics loved Goldie. She even won a best supporting actress Oscar for the role.

Later in 1970, Goldie starred with Peter Sellers in *There's a Girl in My Soup*. As in her first two films, Goldie played a perky and somewhat ditzy woman. However, she began to change her image from silly to serious with her next film. In 1972, she teamed up with Warren Beatty in the movie *Dollars*. In the film, Hawn and Beatty's characters break into a bank in Germany and steal more than a million dollars from thieves who keep their money there. The thieves find out and chase the pair across Germany.

In 1972, Goldie also starred in *Butterflies Are Free*. In this film, she plays a free-loving hippie who becomes friends with her blind neighbor who lives with her overprotective mother. The movie follows the neighbor, the mom, and Goldie's character as they learn that although they are different, they can discover things about life from each other. Goldie did a good job with the role and received positive reviews.

In 1974, Goldie starred in *The Sugarland Express*, Steven Spielberg's first film as a director. *The Sugarland Express* is Goldie's first truly dramatic role. In the film, Goldie plays a woman who a

Steven Spielberg, the famous director of such classic films as *E.T.*, *Jaws*, and *Saving Private Ryan*, directed Goldie in *The Sugarland Express*. This was Spielberg's first time as a director. Shown here on the film set with actor Michael Sacks, Goldie plays a Texan woman on the run from the law.

court decides is an unfit mother because she has a criminal record. As a result, the state takes her infant son. Goldie's character helps her husband escape from jail to try to get their child back. The couple wind up kidnapping a police officer and making him drive them to Sugarland, the town where their son is living. Police follow them, and they become celebrities as the media get involved in the chase. Goldie did a wonderful job playing a woman who is desperate to get her son back.

Goldie's Career Continues

After *The Sugarland Express*, Goldie's career was well under way. She continued starring in movies in the next few years. In 1974, Goldie starred in *The Girl from Petrovka*. In 1975, she once again teamed up with Warren Beatty in *Shampoo*. In 1978, she had the lead role in the popular romantic comedy *Foul Play* with Chevy Chase.

Throughout the 1980s and 1990s, Goldie was in many films, including *Private Benjamin* in 1980. This was Goldie's first time as an executive producer.

In the movie, Goldie plays Judy Benjamin, a rich and spoiled woman who always had a man to take care of her. When her husband dies on their wedding night, Judy joins the army. At first, Private Benjamin is helpless and can't do anything. By the end of the movie however, Judy is transformed into an independent woman who is capable of making her own decisions. *Private Benjamin* was a popular movie and Goldie was nominated for an Oscar for her role.

Goldie's Practice

Goldie describes herself as a "Jewish Buddhist." She says that her general happiness comes from meditating every day and practicing yoga. She usually makes a trip to India once a year and has an "India Room" in her home where she meditates.

Goldie says she will never marry Kurt Russell. She told *Hello!* magazine that "Marriage is a form of ownership." She continues, "I don't like fusion. I think it's dangerous. I think you lose your personal power." However, both Goldie and Kate believe in commitment. Kate has told reporters the story of Kurt giving Goldie a ring and telling her and the children that he wasn't going anywhere. Kate says that she believed him, and Goldie and Kurt have been together ever since.

Wearing her usual friendly and radiant grin, Goldie, along with her daughter, Kate, and son Oliver, arrives at the world premier of *Overboard*. Goldie and partner Kurt Russell both star in this 1987 romantic comedy.

In 1992, Goldie starred in *Housesitter*, a comedy with Steve Martin. That same year, she also starred in *CrissCross* and *Death Becomes Her*. *CrissCross* is a drama about a mother on welfare who is struggling to raise her son in a dangerous area of Key West, Florida. *Death Becomes Her* was a popular film featuring actors Meryl Streep and Bruce Willis.

After finishing the filming of *Death Becomes Her*, Goldie took a four-year break from acting to take care of her mother who was ill. In

1996, she returned to acting with *The First Wives Club* starring Bette Midler and Diane Keaton. Later that year, she sang and danced for the first time in years in *Everyone Says I Love You*. Goldie also starred in *The Banger Sisters* with Susan Sarandon in 2002.

> ## Goldie at the Forefront
>
> In 1997, Goldie was the first female actress and producer to be honored by the American Museum of the Moving Image in New York City.

Goldie has also produced numerous television and film projects including *My Blue Heaven* and *Overboard,* which she starred in with her partner, Kurt Russell. And in 1997, Goldie directed for the first time. The project was *Hope*, a TV movie for Turner Network Television. Since then, Goldie has continued producing television movies and films.

Personal Life

Goldie has been married and divorced twice, but she has been actor Kurt Russell's partner since 1982. The pair met while filming *The One and Only, Genuine, Original Family Band* in 1968. However, they started dating while filming *Swing Shift* in 1982. Goldie has two children, Oliver and Kate Hudson, from her second marriage to comedian Bill Hudson. She also has one child, Wyatt Russell, from her relationship with Kurt. Her most famous offspring is Kate Hudson. Oliver Hudson is also an actor, writer, and director.

CHAPTER 2

LIKE MOTHER, LIKE DAUGHTER

Kate Hudson was born on April 19, 1979, in Los Angeles. Bill Hudson and Goldie Hawn divorced eighteen months after Kate was born. Kate has called Kurt Russell "pop" since he and Goldie started dating when Kate was four.

Friends, family, and work associates have nothing but praise for Kate. Her good looks, work ethic, and upbeat personality are probably the reason she is so well liked. Directors, actors, and producers who have worked with Kate often talk about the fact that she can light up a room. Both Goldie and Kate are very likable and have positive energy that attracts people to them. Kate also works hard and completely throws herself into whatever character she is playing.

Kate's Goal

It was always very important to Kate to be in show business and to do it without relying on the fame of her parents. She wanted to prove herself as an actress

Here, Kate Hudson and friends celebrate the launch of designer Tommy Hilfiger's 1997 jeans collection. One of Kate's earliest jobs was modeling for the Hilfiger line of clothing. She appeared in several advertisements for the company.

Athletic Kate

Kate Hudson played varsity soccer in high school and has taken dance lessons since she was a little girl.

without favors from Goldie and Kurt or their friends. Although Kate never wanted to depend on her parents' fame, being around them is part of what inspired her to become an actress. She got her first taste of show business by seeing Goldie's and Kurt's lives firsthand. Kate's initial experience with moviemaking was in 1986 when her mom was making *Wildcats*. Kate was a stand-in for the seven-year-old girl who played Goldie's daughter in the film.

Kate has always said that she wanted to act. She starred in her first play, *Alice in Wonderland*, when she was six. When she was eleven, she told her mom about her dreams. Goldie wasn't happy to hear about Kate's plans but she wanted to support her daughter. Accordingly, Goldie took the eleven-year-old on an audition. Kate didn't think much of it at the time, but now she feels the story is a perfect example of her mom supporting her daughter's desires over her own.

Kate acted in a few more plays while she was in high school at Crossroads School of Arts and Sciences in Santa Monica, California. At sixteen, she auditioned for a part in the film *Escape from L.A.* After the *Escape from L.A.* experience, Kate became more serious about acting. With the support of her parents, Kate started going on auditions. In 1996, she landed a part on the TV series *Party of Five*. However, the character Kate played was in only one episode. Kate continued to look for projects and got another spot on a TV show called *EZ Streets* in 1997.

After graduating from high school, Kate was accepted to the Tisch School of Drama at New York University, which has a very good reputation. Goldie and Kurt hoped that she would attend because they wanted Kate to finish her schooling before starting an acting career. Instead, Kate persuaded them to let her hold off on college for a year. Then, she moved to Hollywood, got an agent, and started looking for work. And in fact, in 1998, Kate made it to the silver screen in a

Famous Friends

Liv Tyler and Kate Hudson attended school together when they were children. They are still friends.

small independent film named *Desert Blue*. That same year, she was also in *Ricochet River*. Both *Desert Blue* and *Ricochet River* are small films that were not widely seen. Nonetheless, Kate received good reviews from critics for both films.

In 1999, Kate was in a comedy called *200 Cigarettes*. *200 Cigarettes* received poor reviews but had a popular cast and was widely seen. The cast included Christina Ricci, Martha Plimpton, Courtney Love, Ben Affleck, Casey Affleck, and Dave Chappelle. Although the movie was considered mediocre at best, Kate got positive attention from viewers and critics for her performance. The film is about a party that takes place in New York City on New Year's Eve, 1981. Kate plays an innocent young woman who is on a bad date and winds up at the party.

The following year, Kate was in four films: *About Adam*, *Gossip*, *Almost Famous*, and *Dr. T & the Women*. In *About Adam*, she plays a woman who falls in love with a man and brings him home to meet her family. Everyone winds up falling in love with her boyfriend, who charms whomever he meets. The film was not popular with audiences, but film critics felt that Kate's performance was very good. *Gossip* is a drama about a group of spoiled first-year college students who decide to start a false rumor as part of their final papers. *Gossip* was another small film that received poor reviews. And *Dr. T & the Women* was a well-liked mainstream film. In it, Kate

Seeing Yourself Everywhere!

Kate had no idea that a close-up of her face was going to be on the *Almost Famous* promotional poster. Kate was staying with her parents during filming, and Goldie was the first person to see the poster when it arrived at their home. Goldie called her daughter as soon as she opened the package and saw what image they had chosen.

plays Dr. T's daughter. Dr. T is played by Richard Gere. Kate's character gets married, and there is a lot of stress and craziness leading up to the wedding ceremony. The cast includes many famous actors including Shelley Long, Farrah Fawcett, Helen Hunt, and Liv Tyler.

Kate's big break came in 2000, when she played Penny Lane in *Almost Famous*. Kate got the part after Canadian actress Sarah Polley (who starred in *The Sweet Hereafter* in 1997 and *Go* in 1999) dropped out of the film. Originally, Kate had a much smaller role, but when Polley dropped out, Kate told director Cameron Crowe that she could really see herself in the role of Penny Lane. Crowe wasn't sure but ultimately let Kate read for the part. After much convincing, he cast Kate as Penny Lane, one of the main characters in the film.

Kate wowed critics and viewers alike with her performance as a free-spirited rock-and-roll groupie. *Almost Famous* was very popular, and as a result, Kate became a household name. She was nominated for an Academy Award and won a Golden Globe for supporting actress.

The film was partially autobiographical for director Cameron Crowe. The plot is about a fifteen-year-old teen, played by Patrick Fugit, who wants to be a music journalist. He lies about his experience and age and gets an assignment to write an article about a rock-and-roll band. Kate's character, Penny Lane, hangs out with the band and

Kate won the 2001 Golden Globe Award for best supporting actress for her role in *Almost Famous*. Tom Cruise, the famous actor of such films as *Vanilla Sky*, *A Few Good Men*, and *Mission Impossible*, presented her with the award. In this photograph, Tom is sharing the spotlight with an extremely happy Kate.

sometimes dates the lead singer. With the help of Penny, the journalist meets the lead singer and joins the band on tour. Lots of crazy things happen along the way, but *Almost Famous* is mostly a coming-of-age story about young people learning about life.

Kate didn't win an Academy Award for *Almost Famous*. However, she has never felt disappointed. She is trying to build a career that will last. Kate does not want to be popular for a few years

and then forgotten. She told the *Calgary Sun* that when she didn't win the award, Kurt "kissed me and whispered: 'Now you can have a career.' It was a beautiful gesture and so wise and knowing of him." Kate is grateful that she has parents who taught her that there are more important things than awards.

Back to Work

After *Almost Famous*, Kate took some time off from acting. She came back to the screen with *The Four Feathers* in 2002. *The Four Feathers* is a drama about the British army at war in Sudan in the 1890s. In fact, Kate turned down the role of Mary Jane Watson in *Spider-Man* in order to be in *The Four Feathers*.

In 2003, Kate was back to working full-time. She starred in three movies: *Alex and Emma*, *How to Lose a Guy in 10 Days*, and *Le Divorce*. *Alex and Emma* is a comedy starring Luke Wilson. Wilson plays Alex, a writer who needs to get his book finished within a month. He is suffering from writer's block and doesn't have a computer. He hires Emma, played by Kate Hudson, to help him type it. As Alex tells her his book, Emma tells him her opinion. As a result, they wind up writing the book together, and Emma becomes a character in the book. *Alex and Emma* received mostly poor reviews, however, most critics though Kate did a good job in the role. They just felt that the movie was flat.

How to Lose a Guy in 10 Days is also a romantic comedy. Kate got the part after actress Gwyneth Paltrow dropped out. Kate plays a magazine writer whose assignment is to date a man and do everything wrong—act jealous and talk in baby talk. The assignment is to record his reaction to her bad behavior and see how long it takes until he breaks up with her. Of course, in movies things don't happen

Kate follows in stepfather Kurt's stuntman footsteps. Here, on the set of *How to Lose a Guy in 10 Days*, she rides a Triumph Bonneville, a classic British motorcycle.

like they do in real life. In the movie, Matthew McConaughey plays a man who has just bet that he can make a woman fall in love with him in ten days. Kate's character picks McConaughey for her experiment and lots of silliness follows. Kate keeps acting like an airhead but McConaughey doesn't break up with her because he wants to win his bet. Both the movie and Kate's performance received good reviews.

Le Divorce, a comedy that takes place in Paris, was released in 2003. In the film, Kate Hudson plays actress Naomi Watts's sister.

Watts is an American married to a rich French man in Paris. Her husband leaves her for another woman while she is pregnant, so her sister flies from California to Paris to help her through her pregnancy. Kate's character dates many men and learns about France in this comedy. Unfortunately, the film received poor reviews.

Raising Helen, Kate's next film, was released in May 2004. In the film, Kate plays a woman named Helen Harris. Helen works for a big-time modeling firm in New York City, and she loves her life. She goes to lots of fancy parties, stays out late, and makes enough money to do whatever she wants. The film focuses on how Helen's life changes once she becomes responsible for raising her sister's three children.

Currently, Kate is filming a thriller called *Skeleton Key* with actors John Hurt and Peter Sarsgaard. She plays a woman who is caring for the home of an elderly couple and starts to discover some scary secrets. *Skeleton Key* is set in New Orleans, Louisiana, and should be released sometime in 2005.

Kate is gearing up to start filming the first movie that she will also produce. In *Can You Keep a Secret?* Kate plays a marketing executive who tells all her secrets to a stranger next to her on a plane when she thinks the plane is going to crash. She survives the flight but doesn't know that the stranger actually owns the company she works for. *Can You Keep a Secret?* should start filming in 2005.

Personal Life

Kate had a big year in 2000. She was in four films and won the public's heart as Penny Lane in *Almost Famous*. To round out the year, Kate married Chris Robinson on New Year's Eve. Robinson was the lead singer of the rock group the Black Crowes. The Black Crowes have since disbanded, and Robinson is working on his solo career. Kate

Shown here at the premiere of her 2003 film *Le Divorce*, Kate is pregnant with her first child. Ever fashionable, even while pregnant, Kate chose to wear a stunningly textured dress by the well-known Italian fashion designer Missoni.

and Chris had their first child, a boy named Ryder Russell Robinson, on January 7, 2004. The couple chose Russell as Ryder's middle name to honor Kurt Russell. Kate is now very busy juggling her film career with being a wife and mom, as well as her relationship with her parents and siblings.

CHAPTER 3

ONE BIG, HAPPY FAMILY

Kate's family was rather large when she was growing up. There was her mom and Kurt. There was Oliver, her brother. There was Boston Russell, Kurt Russell's son from a previous relationship. And in 1986, Goldie gave birth to Wyatt Russell. All this meant that there were usually four children running around and two adults who were steadily making films.

One would think that Kate's childhood would have been hectic with all kinds of show business going on around her. But even with all the action and excitement that comes with having two famous parents, her family was very close and had a fairly normal home life.

When the children were young, Goldie and Kurt would organize their schedules so that one of them was always home with the kids. They tried to make show business a minor part of their lives. In 2004, Kate told ABC's *Primetime*, "My mother and Kurt . . . never focused on that part of their lives, like a lot of people can . . . They were very adamant

Kurt, Goldie, and the three kids, Oliver, Kate, and Boston (Kurt's son from a previous marriage), pose for a group photo at the premiere of Kurt's 1997 film, *Breakdown*. In this action-packed movie, Kurt plays a man searching for his missing wife.

Advice from Mom

Kate took 2001 off from acting. Part of the reason was a suggestion from Goldie to give some time to her new marriage. For both Goldie and Kate, family is the top priority.

[certain] about the importance of their children coming first."

Kate has said that while growing up, she didn't know that her parents were famous. On contactmusic.com, Kate says, "We were a regular family. Goldie Hawn to me is just my mom, and the Goldie Hawn you know is very different to the one I know." The first time Kate realized her parents were famous was when she was four and Kurt took the family out for her mom's thirty-seventh birthday. After dinner, Kurt snuck the family out the back door to avoid a mob of photographers. As Kate recalls, it didn't work. "I remember running screaming to the car. I was terrified, because I didn't know what these people wanted."

Fame aside, Kate always felt safe when growing up. Goldie, Kate, and the rest of the family are still very close. Kate also tries to make her own home safe and keep her family's strong sense of togetherness intact. In 2001, Kate told *B Magazine UK,* "My family life is so important to me because my parents never brought Hollywood into our home. That's why home is sacred, and a place where we can all go and have the best time hanging out together."

Goldie and Kurt arrive at the 2004 American Film Institute Lifetime Achievement Awards ceremony to honor Meryl Streep. Streep, who is famous for her roles in films such as *Silkwood, Sophie's Choice,* and *The Bridges of Madison County,* is considered by many film critics and reviewers to be the greatest living film actress.

A Special Request

Goldie and Kurt's son, Wyatt, has told his parents that they are not allowed to attend his hockey games. Goldie and Kurt respect Wyatt's request. They say they understand that it is difficult to have famous parents.

Lots of Encouragement

Everyone in the family talks about how smart, open, loving, and upbeat their siblings, children, and parents are. Kate has said that Goldie and Kurt are supportive of all of their children. Oliver, Goldie's oldest child, is an actor, writer, and director. Boston studies politics and Buddhism. Wyatt, Goldie and Kurt's child together, is working hard to become a professional hockey player.

In 2003, Goldie and Kurt moved to Vancouver, British Columbia, so that Wyatt could pursue his hockey career. In 2004, Kurt told *USA Today*, "We uprooted a year and a half ago, but not for hockey. We did it for an individual with a dream and a desire, and he deserved the opportunity." Goldie also feels that Kate and her husband, Chris Robinson, are a perfect fit. Chris has become a part of the family. Kate often jokes that her husband speaks to her mom more often than she does.

The Center

Goldie has tried very hard to make her life happy and peaceful and place her family at the center of it all. In 1999, Goldie told the *Toronto Sun*, "Life, how you live and breathe and care for your family, is really what makes you whole." Goldie also says she has always felt that she had the power to make her dreams happen. She knew she had to work hard for what she wanted, and she has. On Jewishpeople.net,

Goldie and Kate party at the 1997 premiere of *Hope*, a made-for-TV movie that was also Goldie's first directorial effort. *Hope*, a family drama set in a small town, deals with racism in the American South. The movie earned Goldie several positive reviews.

Goldie says, "It's hard for any woman. Women run households, they raise children, they have to be very, very tough. I always saw my mother working, so I never grew up thinking that a man would take care of me, ever."

Kate has a huge amount of admiration for her mother. She feels she has learned a lot from her about working hard profession-ally and personally. Everyone who works with Kate says she is very

Coincidences

In September 2002, Goldie's film, *The Banger Sisters*, and Kate's film, *The Four Feathers*, came out on the same day.

dedicated and puts a lot of effort into creating a believable character. Kate has said she knew that her mother would support her in anything she did, as long as she was serious about it.

Similarities

Even though Kate's hesitation to be in her mom's shadow caused her to stay away from acting projects with her mom, there are still similarities between the two women— as individuals and as actresses. Kate and Goldie both have open, upbeat personalities. They also have a lot of charisma and are energetic and positive. This could just be the image they show the public, but most accounts of the two women from friends confirm that both women are like this in real life as well. Goldie and Kate also have similar smiles and laughs.

Kate Hudson says that becoming famous has brought her and her mom closer together. Kate told *ABC News* that after *Almost Famous* came out, Goldie said, "I never thought there would be somebody in my life who I could really know understood some of the things that I went through." Kate also admitted to *ABC News* that having a famous mother isn't always easy. "It's a difficult thing when you're going through puberty and you're looking at your mother and she's so gorgeous and everybody loves her and everybody wants her. And you're kind of looking at yourself going, 'What about me?'" However, Kate is quick to add that having a famous mother was not much of a problem overall.

Goldie, Kurt, Chris, and Kate pose for the press at the 2002 premiere of *The Banger Sisters*. Goldie stars opposite Susan Sarandon (*Thelma and Louise*, *Dead Man Walking*, and *Bull Durham*) in this sentimental comedy about two best friends who grow apart and then reconnect after twenty years.

Business Collaborations

Kurt Russell, Goldie Hawn, Kate Hudson, and Oliver Hudson also work together. They own a production company called Cosmic Entertainment. Currently, Cosmic Entertainment is producing numerous projects for television and film.

CHAPTER 4

CURRENT PROJECTS

Goldie is finishing up a personal memoir titled *Higher Up Near Heaven*. The book is about her journey to fulfillment. In it, she writes about her life, from childhood to present day, and what she has learned. *Higher Up Near Heaven* is scheduled to be published in 2005. Goldie also directed, produced, and starred in her own project titled *Ashes to Ashes*. She wrote the screenplay with Jeremy Pikser. The film is about a woman who travels from India to Nepal with her husband's ashes but loses them along the way.

Ashes to Ashes was filmed in India. In fact, Goldie travels to India often. In 1996, she went there to film *In the Wild: The Elephants of India with Goldie Hawn*. *In the Wild* is a PBS documentary about Asian elephants. Goldie practices Buddhism and follows the teachings of the spiritual leader the Dalai Lama, who is originally from Tibet but has been exiled to India since 1959. The Dalai Lama is in exile because he and his followers rebelled against the Chinese government that rules Tibet. Goldie has done many things to help the Dalai Lama and his followers. For

Goldie arrives at a school in India to watch a traditional Tibetan dance performance. After the 1950 Chinese occupation, the former Tibetan government fled to India where it remains today, awaiting the chance to return to and govern Tibet. Goldie is a long-time supporter of Tibet's bid for freedom.

The audience at the Tibetan Children's Village School in India includes Goldie and, wearing a black shirt and seated to the left, Richard Gere (who is also an active supporter of a free Tibet). The dance was in honor of a conference to bring together Western science and Buddhist philosophy.

example, in 2003, Goldie Hawn and famous actor Richard Gere gave $1 million to Tibetans living in exile in India.

Goldie also tours and lectures about her life and what she's learned about being happy. She speaks at universities and lecture halls throughout the country. One of the things she speaks about is the Bright Light Foundation, which she started. The Bright Light

Foundation researches and develops teaching programs for children. Goldie is dedicated to creating a more peaceful world and feels that giving children more attention is a good way to start. She also believes that laughter is an important part of life and can heal almost anything.

To that end, she is developing a Traveling Museum of Laughter, which is an exhibit that will try to educate the public about the scientific and emotional importance of laughter.

Goldie's Philosophy

"I made defined choices and I balance my life with other things like motherhood, my family, and trying to travel and learn new things. My life has not been about this business. It's obviously supported me, but when you talk about lofty goals, I love life and the idea of grinding these movies out is just not me."
—Goldie Hawn,
N-Zone Magazine

Kate Now

Kate Hudson works hard just like her mom. She also understands that she has to make her life apart from work fulfilling. Kate has learned that you can't take yourself too seriously in show business. She tries to pick parts that she loves and wants to work with people she admires. Kate feels that being proud of your accomplishments is more important than being in a blockbuster movie.

Because of this, Kate tries to pick her projects wisely. She is producing and starring in *Can You Keep a Secret?*, a romantic comedy based on the novel of the same name by Sophie Kinsella. Kate says she would also like to direct. She produced a television show titled *I Do, I Did, Now What*. *I Do, I Did, Now What* is based on the best-selling

Kate and costars enjoy themselves on the set of *Raising Helen*. In this 2004 comedy, Kate's character must raise her sister's three children after her sister dies in a car accident. Although Kate's performance was well-received by the critics, most reviews found the movie rather dull.

novel by Jenny Lee. The show is about what happens to couples after they get married. Kate and Cosmic Entertainment developed the show's pilot.

In 2004, Kate had a lot going on. *Raising Helen*, co-starring Joan Cusack and John Corbett, was released on May 28. *Raising Helen* is a comedy/drama. In the film, Kate plays a partying modeling agency executive living in New York City who suddenly must care for her sister and brother-in-law's three children. Besides having to do all the press associated with releasing *Raising Helen*, Kate is also busy working on *Skeleton Key*. *Skeleton Key* was written by Ehren Kruger. Kruger also wrote *The Ring* and *Scream 3*. *Skeleton Key* was scheduled to be filmed in 2003 and released in 2004 but Kate became pregnant, so the film's producers and director waited until Kate had her child to start filming. It will now be released in 2005.

Of course, with an infant at home and a super-busy career, Kate has more than enough to do. For both Kate and Goldie, the most important thing is family. Kate and her husband Chris have moved from New York to Malibu, California, to be closer to Goldie and Kurt's home in California. Kate often speaks about the importance that Goldie and Kurt placed on family when she was growing up. In 2003, she told the *Daily News*, "I learned from growing up with them to do your job the best you can, and go home and concern yourself with your home life. That's where people blossom as people."

Goldie Hawn

1968	• The One and Only, Genuine, Original Family Band
1969	• Cactus Flower
1970	• There's a Girl in My Soup
1972	• Dollars, Butterflies Are Free
1974	• The Sugarland Express, The Girl from Petrovka
1975	• Shampoo
1976	• The Dutchess and the Dirtwater Fox
1978	• Foul Play
1979	• Lovers and Liars
1980	• Private Benjamin, Seems Like Old Times
1982	• Best Friends
1984	• Swing Shift, Protocol
1986	• Wildcats
1987	• Overboard
1990	• Bird on a Wire
1991	• Deceived
1992	• CrissCross, Housesitter, Death Becomes Her
1996	• The First Wives Club, Everyone Says I Love You
1999	• The Out-of-Towners
2000	• Town and County
2002	• The Banger Sisters

Kate Hudson

1998	• Desert Blue, Ricochet River
1999	• 200 Cigarettes
2000	• About Adam, Gossip, Almost Famous, Dr. T & the Women
2002	• The Four Feathers
2003	• Alex and Emma, How to Lose a Guy in 10 Days, Le Divorce
2004	• Raising Helen
2005	• Skeleton Key (scheduled release)

agent Someone who helps an actor get work.

blooper A mistake that is often funny.

cast The group of actors that works on a film or play.

charisma A quality that makes you attractive to others.

cue cards Cards that actors use to read their lines.

debut The first time that someone or something appears in public.

ditzy Silly.

documentary A nonfiction film.

drama A film or play that is very emotional and often sad.

executive producer Someone who provides the money for, and is in charge of, the making of a film.

exile To not be allowed to live in a certain place.

fusion The coming together of something.

gossip To talk about someone's secrets.

groupie A fan who follows a band around.

independent film A film made by a small company.

mainstream The prevailing opinion.

meditation Concentrating on one thing deeply and for a long time in a quiet space for the purpose of reaching a calm or spiritual state.

PBS A group of public television stations that creates, produces, and airs programs.

pilot The first episode of a series made with the purpose of getting a sponsor.

private Not in public.

recruit Someone who is new to a field.

suburb An area where people live close to a city.

yoga A type of exercise that helps a person get in touch with his or her mind and body.

Web Sites

Due to the changing nature of Internet links, the Rosen Publishing Group, Inc., has developed an online list of Web sites related to the subject of this book. This site is updated regularly. Please use this link to access the list.

http://www.rosenlinks.com/fafa/ghkh

Berman, Connie. *Solid Goldie*. Columbus, Ohio: Fireside Publishing, 1981.

Costello, Patricia. *Female Fitness Stars of TV and the Movies: Featuring Profiles of Cher, Goldie Hawn, Lucy Lawless, and Demi Moore*. Hockessin, DE: Mitchell Lane Publishers, 2000.

Shapiro, Marc. *Pure Goldie: The Life and Career of Goldie Hawn*. Secaucus, NJ: Carol Publishing Group, 1998.

BIBLIOGRAPHY

A Class Celebs Web site. "The (Almost) Famous Kate Hudson." 2000. Retrieved May 18, 2004 (http://www.aclasscelebs.com/kateh/almost.htm).

ABC News Web site. "Golden Child." Retrieved May 18, 2004 (http://abcnews.go.com/sections/primetime/DailyNews/kate_hudson_030130.html).

Borden, Anne S. Jewish People.Net Web site. "Goldie Hawn." Retrieved May 18, 2004 (http://www.jewishpeople.net/goldiehawn1.html).

Contact Music Web site. "Goldie Hawn's Just My Mum." Retrieved May 18, 2004 (http://www.contactmusic.com/new/xmlfeed.nsf/mndwebpages/kate%20hudson.%20.goldie%20hawn.S%20just%20my%20mum).

Hello! Magazine Web Site. "Goldie Hawn." Retrieved May 18, 2004 (http://www.hellomagazine.com/profiles/goldiehawn).

Hobson, Louis B. Jam! Showbiz Web site. "Mother Knows Best." 2002. Retrieved May 18, 2004 (http://www.canoe.ca/JamMoviesArtistsH/hudson_kate.html).

Mills, Nancy. *Daily News* Web site. "Kate Hudson Can't 'Lose.'" 2003. Retrieved May 18, 2004 (http://www.nydailynews.com/entertainment/movies/story/56681p-53044c.html).

Siegler, Bonnie. *N-Zone Magazine* Web site. "Goldie Hawn Is One of the Banger Sisters." Retrieved May 18, 2004 (http://www.atnzone.com/moviezone/features/goldiehawn.shtml).

Slotek, Jim. Jam! Showbiz Web site. "In Her Goldie Years." 1999. Retrieved May 18, 2004 (http://www.canoe.ca/JamMoviesArtistsH/hawn_goldie.html).

Thomas, Karen. *USA Today* Web site. "'Coach' Russell Slides Easily Into the Role." 2004. Retrieved May 18, 2004 (http://www.usatoday.com/life/movies/news/2004-02-05-russell-hockey-dad_x.htm).

INDEX

About the Author

Lisa Modifica is from New York City and likes to read, dance, cook, and eat cookies.

Photo Credits

Cover (left), p. 31 © Frank Trapper/Corbis; cover (right) © Rufus F. Folkks/Corbis; pp. 1 (left and right), 23, 27, 28, 35, 36, 38 © AP/Wide World Photos; p. 4 © Lisa O'Connor/Zuma/Corbis; p. 6 © Photo B. D. V./Corbis; p. 8 © Douglas Kirkland/Corbis; pp. 11, 16 © Bettmann/Corbis; p. 12 © Corbis; p. 14 © Sunset Boulevard/Corbis Sygma; p. 18 © Steve Azzara/Corbis; p. 25 © Steve Sands/New York Newswire/Corbis; p. 33 © Tama Herrick/Corbis; p. 40 © Ron Batzdorff/Touchstone Pictures/Keline Howard/Corbis.

Designer: Nelson Sá; **Editor:** Annie Sommers;
Photo Researcher: Nelson Sá